{geography focus}

ENVIRONMENT AT RISK

{the effects of pollution}

Louise Spilsbury

www.raintreepublishers.co.uk
Visit our website to find out more information about **Raintree** books.

To order:
☎ Phone 44 (0) 1865 888112
▤ Send a fax to 44 (0) 1865 314091
▱ Visit the Raintree Bookshop at **www.raintreepublishers.co.uk** to browse our catalogue and order online.

First published 2006 by Heinemann Library a division of Harcourt Education Australia, 20 Thackray Road, Port Melbourne Victoria 3207 Australia (a division of Reed International Books Australia Pty Ltd, ABN 70 001 002 357). Visit the Heinemann Library website at www.heinemannlibrary.com.au

Published in Great Britain in 2006 by Raintree, Halley Court, Jordan Hill, Oxford OX2 8EJ, part of Harcourt Education www.raintreepublishers.co.uk

 A Reed Elsevier company

© Reed International Books Australia Pty Ltd 2006

10 09 08 07 06
10 9 8 7 6 5 4 3 2 1

Editorial: Moira Anderson, Carmel Heron, Diyan Leake, Patrick Catel
Cover, text design & graphs: Marta White
Photo research: Karen Forsythe, Wendy Duncan
Production: Tracey Jarrett, Duncan Gilbert
Map diagrams: Guy Holt
Technical diagrams: Nives Porcellato & Andy Craig

Typeset in 12/17.5 pt Gill Sans Regular
Origination by Modern Age
Printed and bound in Hong Kong, China by South China Printing Company Ltd

The paper used to print this book comes from sustainable resources.

National Library of Australia Cataloguing-in-Publication data:

Spilsbury, Louise.
    Environment at risk : the effects of pollution.

    Includes index.
    For upper primary and lower secondary school students.
    ISBN 1 74070 278 6.

    1. Pollution – Environmental aspects – Juvenile literature.
    1. Title. (Series : Spilsbury, Louise. Geography focus).

363.73

Acknowledgements
The publisher would like to thank the following for permission to reproduce copyright material: AAP/AFP Image: p. **32**, /EPA/Lavandeira Jr Efa: p. **24**, /Wildlight: p. **38**; APL/Jonathan Blair: p. **22** (right), /Corbis /Bettmann: p. **26**, /Ecoscene/Andy Hibbert: p. **12**, /Ric Ergenbright: p. **20**, /Wolfgang Kaehler: p. **4**, /Sally A. Morgan: p. **28**, /Charles E. Rotkin: p. **8**, /Stapleton Shannon: p. **14**, /Liba Taylor: p. **18**, /Robert Weight: p. **36**; Fairfax Photos/Nicole Emanuel: p. **10**; Getty Images/ AFP/Fayez Nureldine: p. **30**, /Taxi: p. **7**; Greenpeace/Horneman: p. **41**; NASA: p. **11**; Naturepl.com/Colin Seddon: p. **34**; Newspix: p. **43**; SeaPics.com/Doug Perrine: p. **37**; Photolibrary.com/Index Stock: p. **19**, /Science Photo Library: pp. **16, 42**. All other images PhotoDisc.

Cover photograph of fish and inset photograph of a rubbish dump reproduced with permission of PhotoDisc.

Every attempt has been made to trace and acknowledge copyright. Where an attempt has been unsuccessful, the publisher would be pleased to hear from the copyright owner so any omission or error can be rectified.

Disclaimer
All the Internet addresses (URLs) given in this book were valid at the time of going to press. However, due to the dynamic nature of the Internet, some addresses may have changed, or sites may have changed or ceased to exist since publication. While the author and publishers regret any inconvenience this may cause readers, no responsibility for any such changes can be accepted by either the author or the publishers.

{contents}

Words that are printed in bold, **like this**, are explained in the Glossary on page 46.

{our world}

Our world is a giant ball of rock floating in space, but it is not empty and lifeless like every other planet we know about. There are millions of different types of living things in our world, from the tallest trees to the tiniest insects. What makes our planet different is the **environment** – the air, water, land, and other parts of our surroundings that give us all life. The trouble is that people are damaging parts of the environment. When we put the environment at risk, we affect the lives not only of plants and animals, but also of ourselves.

Interdependent

Living things in the environment are **interdependent**. This means they rely on each other in different ways. For example, herons visit a watery marsh to eat some of the frogs that live there. Putting this environment at risk would affect marsh life. If people accidentally spilled poison in the marsh, all the frogs might die and the herons would then go hungry. But the poison could also affect people. It might poison their drinking water and also cause other problems. Without frogs, the mosquitoes they usually eat would increase in number and then become a nuisance, by biting people living near the marsh.

Many other kinds of plants and animals thrive upon and alongside the trees in a healthy forest environment like this.

Six of the worst environmental disasters

This is a world map showing where several major disasters have affected environments since 1980. **Pollution** is when part of the environment is poisoned or harmed by human activity. These disasters happened for different reasons and in different ways. After these disasters, pollution had long-lasting effects on the environment.

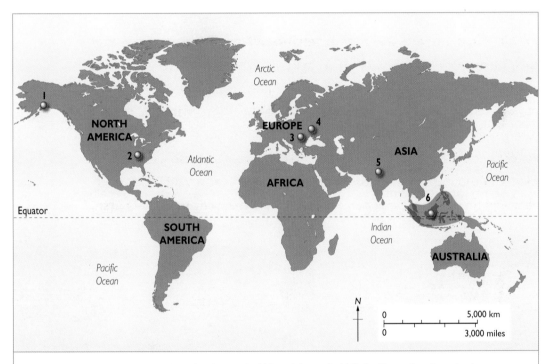

● 1 Alaska, USA, 1989: *Exxon Valdez* oil tanker crashed. The oil that spilled killed millions of marine animals and ruined 2,250 km (1,400 miles) of coastline.

● 2 Kentucky, USA, 2000: Poisonous coal mining waste accidentally spilled, killing all animals in 70 km (40 miles) of rivers.

● 3 Romania, 2000: Mining waste poisoned rivers, killing hundreds of tonnes of fish.

● 4 Ukraine, 1986: Chernobyl power station (see page 34).

● 5 Bhopal, India, 1984: Poisonous gas leak killed 20,000 people, blinded thousands more and poisoned drinking water.

● 6 Indonesia, 1997: Smoke from forest fires mixed with other air pollution, forming an immense cloud of **smog** over Indonesia. The smog caused breathing problems in 70 million people and killed millions of plants.

This world map shows the location of recent environmental disasters.

{risks to the environment}

Some risks to the **environment** are natural and gradual. Throughout the history of the Earth the environment has gradually altered as **climate** has changed. Climate is the usual weather in a place. For example, Antarctica has not always been a cold, icy place. Rocks found there suggest that 50 million years ago it was warm and covered in thick forest. Since then, as the climate has cooled, fewer types of plants and animals have managed to survive in Antarctica. Many have died out or been forced to move elsewhere.

Sudden natural changes

Some natural changes to the environment are sudden. Natural risks include **earthquakes**, **floods** and **volcanoes**. When a volcano goes off or **erupts**, it instantly transforms the environment around it. It may throw tonnes of scalding ash and poisonous gases into the air. Rain eventually washes the ash and gas back to Earth. This chokes and poisons rivers and kills plants and animals. Rivers of red-hot melted rock called lava may rush down slopes of a volcano when it erupts. Lava burns away everything in its path and forms a new layer of rock as it cools.

Mount Pinatubo, the volcano that erupted on Luzon Island in the Philippines in June 1991, killing 200 people and dramatically altering the surrounding environment.

6

Slow and fast pollution

Just like natural risks, **pollution** can change environments gradually or suddenly. For example, each time farmers spray bug-killing chemicals called **pesticides** on their crops, some falls on the soil. When it rains, some of this pesticide is washed from the soil into a nearby river. Gradually the amounts of pesticide in the river grow until they harm the fish and other living things in the river.

Single, sudden pollution events can have equally damaging effects. Imagine a clean river in which a factory dumps tonnes of poisonous chemicals to get rid of them. Within minutes, hours and days, nearly all life in that river environment might be at risk.

Water pollution can have a disastrous effect on wildlife in a river. It can kill off plants that many insects and other animals rely on for food and shelter. It might poison fish directly, or it can kill the small animals that many fish and other river animals feed on.

{ pollution in the atmosphere }

There is a barrier between our planet and space, a bit like the candy coating around a chocolate drop. The barrier, called the **atmosphere**, is made up of layers of air containing different gases. These gases include **oxygen**, which most animals need to breathe. They also include **carbon dioxide**, which green plants need in order to make their own food by **photosynthesis**. The atmosphere is vital for many living things and therefore it is an enormous problem when it gets **polluted**.

FACT!

Fossil fuels formed when the remains of plants and animals that died millions of years ago were trapped under layers of rock. Over time they were crushed and changed into material that will burn to release energy.

Smoke from factories can mix with fog to form giant clouds that trap polluting gases over towns and cities.

What pollutes the atmosphere?

Most pollution in the atmosphere is caused by fossil fuels. People burn fossil fuels, such as oil, coal, and gas, to produce energy. This energy is used to run cars or trains, to light and warm our homes, and to power factory machines. When fossil fuels burn, they release smoke and invisible gases, such as carbon monoxide and nitrogen dioxide. These gases drift up from chimneys and exhaust pipes into the sky and pollute the atmosphere.

Air pollution and population

The world's **population** and the amount of air pollution are changing. The graph below shows that in fact population and pollution are increasing at the same rate. The increase has speeded up since about 1950. It was around this time, after World War II, that more babies started to be born and healthcare improved. The fast-growing population used more fossil fuels than ever before. They burnt more coal in power stations to make electricity to power more machines. They used more petrol to run cars.

FACT!

Pollution affects population. Around 3 million people die each year from the effects of air pollution. This is three times the 1 million who die each year in car accidents.

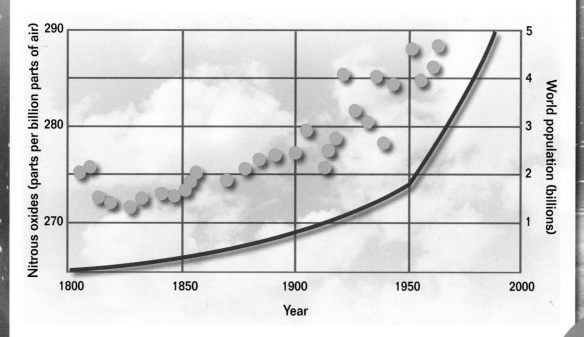

This graph shows rising levels of air pollution (blue dots) over the past 200 years.

{changing atmosphere}

One part of the **atmosphere**, about 40 kilometres (25 miles) above us, is called the **ozone layer**. Ozone is a type of gas. At ground level it is a **polluting** gas. In the sky, however, ozone shields life on Earth from harmful **ultraviolet radiation** from our nearest star, the Sun. In small amounts, this radiation tans our skin, but in large amounts it burns and can cause skin **cancer**.

Disappearing ozone

In 1985, scientists investigating the atmosphere over Antarctica found there was a hole in the ozone layer. During the 1990s another hole appeared over the North Pole too. Scientists believe gases used in refrigerators, aerosol cans, and foam packaging have escaped into the air. These gases have polluted the atmosphere, causing these holes.

This change in the Earth's atmosphere affects all of us. The pollution has seriously reduced the amount of protection the ozone layer can give us. Now we have to protect ourselves from ultraviolet radiation by using sun blocks and keeping out of the Sun. Although the holes will never close, we can protect the remaining ozone layer by using fewer polluting gases.

With growing holes in the ozone layer, we are at greater risk of developing skin cancer. That's why it is vitally important to use suncream and cover up in the sun.

View from space

How do scientists keep track of changes in the ozone layer? One way is to take photos from spacecraft and **satellites** in space. This photo, taken in 2003, shows an enormous hole in the ozone layer. The hole is larger than the combined area of the USA, Canada, and Mexico.

- On the photo you can see South America and Antarctica. The hole almost completely covers Antarctica. People living in the Southern Hemisphere, in countries like New Zealand and Australia, are most in danger from ultraviolet radiation. However, the damage to the ozone layer affects everyone on the planet.

- By comparing this photo with others taken before, the scientists can see that the hole is getting bigger.

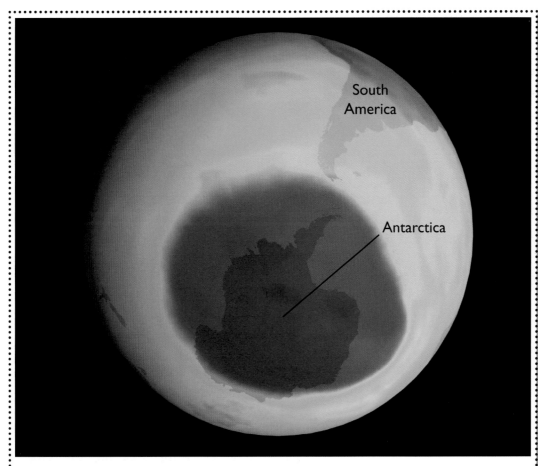

South America

Antarctica

The dark blue area in this picture shows the extent of the hole in the ozone layer above the Earth.

{acid rain}

When **acid rain** falls on Earth it can be very damaging to the **environment**. It washes away some of the nutrients in the soil and this can make it difficult for plants such as trees to grow. The **acid** also damages leaves, so they cannot make food for the trees they grow on by **photosynthesis**. In Europe, the USA, and Japan, large areas of trees have turned brown and died because of acid rain.

Some acid rain runs off land and collects in lakes. Acid lake water damages the sensitive skin of animals, such as fish, snails, and frogs, often killing them. Nearly half of Sweden's 90,000 lakes are too acid for many living things to survive. Water from acid lakes and **reservoirs** is not safe to drink.

What is an acid?

Acids are types of chemicals. Strong acids, such as sulphuric acid, can dissolve metal and burn skin. Weak acids, such as vinegar or cola, can still damage or change the materials they touch. Try putting a coin in a jar of cola and see what happens. (Don't drink the cola afterwards.)

Acid rain can dissolve and wear away hard stone used in buildings and statues.

How does rain become acid?

The story of acid rain begins with air **pollution**. Polluting gases in the air, such as sulphur dioxide, are released when people burn **fossil fuels**. The gases make tiny droplets of water in the air acidic. The acid in the water droplets is usually as strong as lemon juice.

It is cold higher in the **atmosphere**. The droplets group together in clouds to form drops of acid water. The drops eventually fall onto Earth as rain or snow. Acid rain is usually worst near places with lots of factories. However, wind can blow polluting gases from tall chimneys for hundreds of kilometres before they mix with rain. Then remote wild places are also damaged by acid rain.

acidic gases
acid rain
water

This diagram shows how acid rain forms and falls to Earth.

{rising temperatures}

Apart from providing the air we need and protecting us from **ultraviolet radiation**, the **atmosphere** plays another important role. It helps to control the temperature on Earth. Rather like the glass in a greenhouse, the atmosphere lets in heat from the Sun and stops some of it from escaping. It traps heat next to the Earth's surface. The problem is that **pollution** in the atmosphere is making it trap more heat. The polluting gases responsible are **carbon dioxide** and carbon monoxide. They are produced when people burn **fossil fuels**.

A warmer planet

The trapped heat seems to be warming up **climates** around the world. This is called **global warming**. Global warming has lots of effects on parts of the **environment**. In some places, such as in Antarctica or up high mountains, the extra heat is melting ice. In other places new animals, such as disease-carrying insects, are moving in. They are moving in because these places are now warm enough for them to survive. Hotter weather is drying up trees so much that they catch fire far more easily. This means that severe forest fires are more likely.

*Mosquitoes have moved into New York City as the climate has become warmer. Aircraft have been used to spray them with **pesticides**.*

Temperature and sea level

The first graph below shows the global temperature data between 1900 and 2000. The data forms a wiggly line that goes up and down, but generally the line goes up. It shows the temperature has risen by about 1.2 °F (0.6 °C). This may not sound like very much, but it is enough to have some big effects.

The second graph shows how the sea level has risen by about 5 inches (12 centimeters) over the same period of time. This is because the rising temperature has melted some of the polar **ice caps**, adding more water to the world's oceans. If the sea level continues to rise, the sea could **flood** some islands and coastal towns.

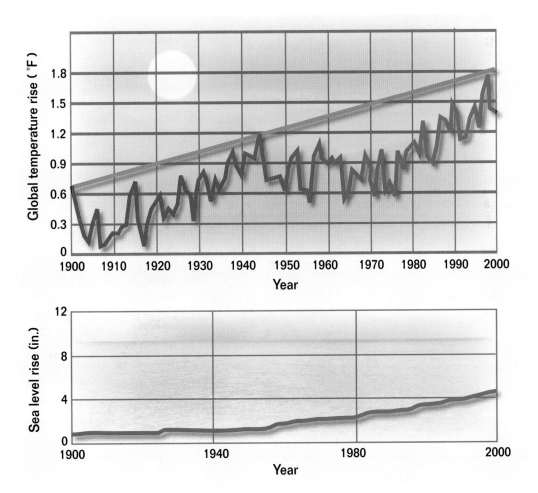

The top graph shows rising global temperatures, while the bottom graph shows the rising sea level.

{traffic pollution}

Travel is easier now than at any point in the history of the Earth. People fly and drive all over the planet. The trouble is that all this traffic is producing **pollution** that damages our world.

Choking cars

Car exhaust fumes affect human health. They contain several poisonous gases but also tiny particles (bits) of soot and dirt. Polluting particles in car fumes clog up people's noses and make their eyes and skin itch. Polluting gases such as nitrogen dioxide and carbon monoxide irritate people's throats and lungs. The irritation can trigger **asthma** attacks in some people with sensitive throats and lungs.

FACT!

There are now over 600 million cars in the world. That is one car for every ten people on Earth. The number of cars is expected to double within the next 30 years.

The problem is made worse because every year there are more and more cars on the roads. Traffic jams happen when roads get clogged up with cars. Some drivers leave their engines on in traffic jams, even though their cars aren't moving. This creates more pollution.

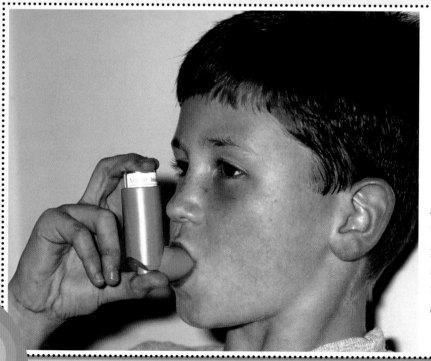

Asthma is made worse by traffic pollution. This child is taking medicines to make his asthma better.

Flying into trouble

Aeroplanes and cars produce about the same amount of air pollution for each kilometre travelled. But planes travel massive distances. One return trip from the UK to the USA produces as much **carbon dioxide** as a whole year of average-length car journeys. Polluting gases released high in the sky damage the **ozone layer** more quickly than gases released at ground level by cars. Contrails, the white lines in the sky where aircraft have flown, group together to form clouds. These clouds and the carbon dioxide made by jet engines trap heat, adding to **global warming**.

Flying more

People are travelling more by plane each year. This graph shows the increase in the numbers of passengers who used airports in the UK from 1980 to 2000. The numbers rose from 50 million in 1980 to 160 million in 2000.

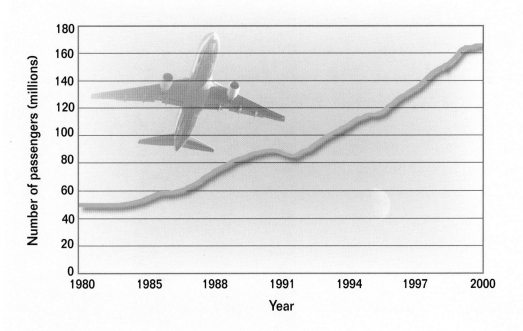

This graph shows increasing numbers of airline passengers in the UK from 1980 to 2000.

{case study}
Tokyo traffic

Tokyo, the capital city of Japan, is a big, growing city. It has been the largest city in the world since the 1960s. If it grows at present rates, by 2015 Tokyo's population will reach nearly 29 million people. That is nearly the number of people living in the whole of Canada in 2004.

In Tokyo, 90 percent of workers travel to and from their offices by train. Despite the fact that so many people use public transport in the city, **pollution** from vehicles is a major problem. Some of the worst pollution is from transport lorries that carry goods into the city.

Solving the problem

The government in Tokyo decided to try to clean up transport lorries. They encouraged lorry makers to make new lorries that are cleaner. These use less fuel and produce less polluting particles in their exhaust smoke. The government also encouraged owners of older lorries to fit special devices to their exhaust pipes. These devices removed some of the particles from the exhaust fumes.

In Tokyo some people wear face masks to stop them breathing in air pollution.

In October 2003, Tokyo's government introduced a new law. Any lorry that dirtied the air too much would not be allowed to drive in Tokyo again. Government inspectors stopped lorries and checked how much pollution they were making. By October 2004, the message had got around that lorries needed to clean up their act. Air measurements around the city showed that Tokyo air contained 14 percent fewer particles from lorry exhausts.

Although things are getting better in Tokyo, it still has air pollution problems. There are fewer particles now, but amounts of some polluting gases have risen because there are more and more cars in Tokyo.

More cars

In 1970 there were 17 million vehicles on Japan's roads. In 2003 there were 74 million vehicles. Of these vehicles, 55 million were cars. The number is set to rise as more families are now buying second or even third cars. The roads in Tokyo are increasingly clogged up.

In Tokyo there are as many as 250 cars per kilometre of road.

{water pollution}

Living things need clean water. Some, like us, need it to drink. Others, like fish, need it to live in. The problem is that people are **polluting** rivers, lakes, and seas, and changing the water **environment** all over the planet.

Water killer

Imagine living by a river or pond that people wash themselves, their animals, and their dirty clothes in, and use as a toilet. **Bacteria** and disease-carrying insects live in and by the water. Yet people collect the filthy water to drink because it is the only water they have. This is what life is really like for over half the people of the world. The more water people drink, the sicker they get.

There are many ways people pollute water. For example, factories pour poisonous chemicals into rivers. Some of these chemicals make people sick and kill fish and other animals that live in water.

FACT!

Every year 5 million people die from diseases such as **diarrhoea** caused by dirty water.

Water is vital for life. In 2003 the first People's World Water Forum stated that everyone should have access to 40 litres (9 gallons) of water a day. Many people who have to collect water from wells like this may not have that much for an entire family.

Polluted seas

About three-fifths of our planet is covered in seawater. Because the oceans are so wide and deep, people think that waste cannot pollute them. They think the problem will just dissolve or float away in the water. But the world's ocean environment is being polluted. Some pollution comes directly from the growing number of cities along the world's coasts. Some pollution washes down rivers into the sea. Some is dumped from ships.

Growing more

Fertilizers are chemicals that farmers spray on soil to make plants grow faster. But when rain washes fertilizers off land into rivers, they pollute the water. The map below shows how much fertilizer different countries put on their farmland in 1998.

- The countries marked purple are those that use most fertilizer per square kilometre. These include Switzerland, the Netherlands, the UK, and Iceland.

- The countries marked light grey are those that use the least fertilizer, such as large parts of Africa.

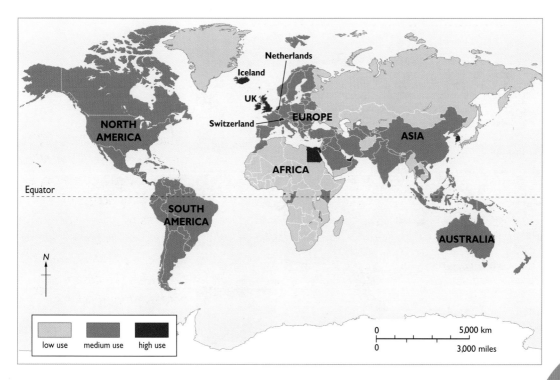

This world map shows fertilizer use in 1998.

{case study}
the Mediterranean

When most people think of the Mediterranean Sea, they think of beautiful coastal villages and swimming in clear turquoise water. What they usually do not imagine is a **polluted** sea that in places is even dangerous to swim in. Some pollution is caused year round by towns, farms, and factories around the Mediterranean coast. But most pollution is caused by tourists.

Tourism pollution

Tourism is a really important industry for Mediterranean countries such as Spain, Italy, Greece, and France. Thousands of people make money when visitors buy their souvenirs, stay in their hotels, or eat in their restaurants. But each summer the number of visitors doubles the coastal **population** of the Mediterranean and this causes problems.

Each extra visitor creates more pollution. For example, waste water from sinks, baths, showers, dishwashers, and toilets is flushed straight into the sea. This **sewage** contains dangerous amounts of **bacteria** that can sometimes cause serious diseases. It also contains chemicals called nitrates. These encourage the growth of green slime in the water, which not only looks bad but can also damage seaweeds and the animals that eat them.

The beaches on the Mediterranean Sea are popular with tourists (left) but much of the extra waste created by tourists flows into the sea (right).

Growing problem

Poisonous substances, such as mercury, dumped in the Mediterranean Sea by factories and ships, are also causing pollution in some parts of the sea. When fish and shellfish eat small amounts of poison it may not harm them. But when seals or people eat lots of fish, the poison can then build up inside them, making them sick.

Sewage map

Two-thirds of the sewage from Mediterranean countries ends up in the sea. That's the weight of seven giant cruise ships each year. The dark blue lines on the map show the parts of the Mediterranean coastline that are most polluted by sewage. You can see that it is not evenly spread out. It collects in certain parts of the coastline. This is partly because this is where there are most tourists. It is also partly because water in the Mediterranean Sea is closed in by land. It does not move around as much as water in oceans. This means the sewage is not washed away from the coast.

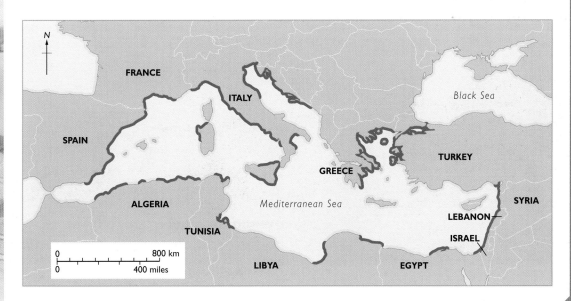

This map of the Mediterranean area shows the most polluted parts of the coast.

{oil pollution}

Oil is often called 'black gold'. It is one of the most important **raw materials** on Earth. Every day, the people around the planet use up massive amounts of oil. We use oil to make lots of things, from the fuel that powers our cars, to the plastic that is shaped into toys and computers.

Fossil fuels

Oil is a **fossil fuel** that has formed naturally over millions of years. It started as the dead remains of tiny animals on ancient sea floors. Over time, the remains got trapped and crushed under layers of rock. The remains turned into black liquid oil. People have to drill through thick layers of rock to get at the oil underneath. Sometimes the rocks are under the oceans or in remote wild places, such as Alaska in the USA.

The oil that is drilled out is transported around the world in **oil tankers** and through pipes. When tankers and pipes leak, the sticky liquid oil can kill animals and plants. It also **pollutes** the places they live in.

In 2002 an ageing oil tanker called Prestige *broke open during storms. It spilled 60,000 tonnes (59,000 tons) of oil into the sea. The oil washed onto the coastlines of France and Spain. It killed many birds and shellfish and ruined beaches.*

Deadly oil spills

Oil spills can happen whenever and wherever oil is drilled, transported, or used. The shaded areas on the map show where oil is drilled. Nearly one-third of all the world's oil comes from Saudi Arabia in the Middle East. The arrows show the routes oil tankers take from these oil-producing areas. The red dots on this map show where some of the worst oil spills have happened since 1960. They are almost all on oil tanker routes. Each spill polluted the environment for wildlife, plants, and people.

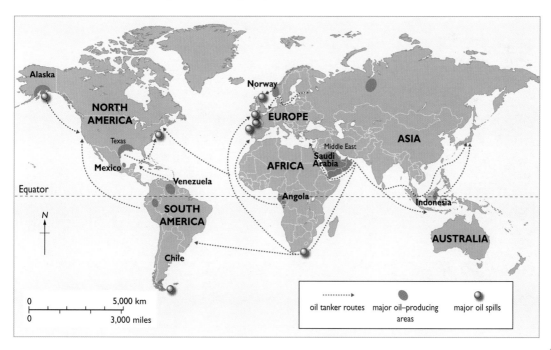

This map shows the sites of the world's major oil spills since 1960.

{the effects of oil pollution}

Oil **pollution** has some very obvious visual effects. Sticky, smelly black oil can be washed onto the sand and rocks of attractive coastlines. Then tourists will not want to visit.

There are also less obvious problems caused by oil pollution. For example, young fish on oil-polluted **reefs** develop diseases and do not grow properly. This reduces the amount of sea fish people and other animals can catch to eat. It costs a lot of money and takes a lot of time to clean up oil pollution.

Floating killer

Oil clogs the feathers or fur of ocean animals, such as seabirds and sea otters. The fur or feathers usually trap air around these animals' bodies, like a quilt. But when they are clogged with oil they cannot help the animals keep warm in the water. Then many die of cold. The oil can weigh the animals down so much that they drown. Animals also get sick when they try to clean off the oil by eating it.

SORRY! BEACH CLOSED FOR THE DAY

Oil pollution has badly affected wildlife and tourism in this coastline environment in Puerto Rico.

Not just tankers!

Big oil spills at sea are the most obvious type of oil pollution in the sea. But this pie chart reveals, surprisingly, that most oil pollution has nothing to do with oil spills from **oil tankers** or pipes. Some oil pollution happens when people clean out ships at sea. Some happens when rain washes oily smoke from the air into the sea. Some happens when oil is drilled from rocks and some when oil naturally seeps from rocks.

The pie chart shows us that well over half of all oil pollution in the world's oceans washes off the land. People cause it by throwing away or spilling waste oil, pouring waste oil down drains or dumping it on land. Oil and petrol drip accidentally from cars and other vehicles. Rain washes this oil off land into rivers and then into seas. Amazingly, the amount of oil washed from just one city with 5 million people is about the same as one large tanker spill.

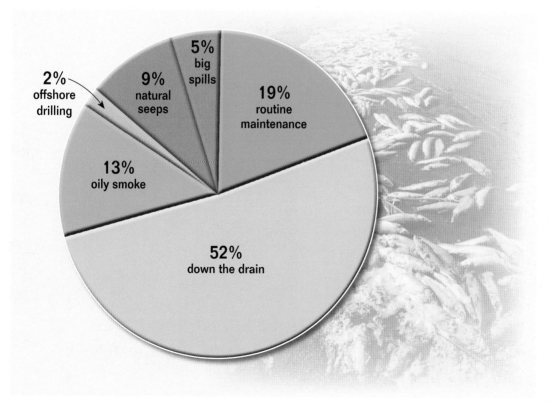

This pie chart shows the sources of oil pollution.

{a load of rubbish}

People around the planet produce enormous amounts of waste. This waste includes the packaging around snacks we buy and the newspapers we have read. It includes the clothes, toys, and mobile phones we have replaced with newer models. How do we get rid of all this waste?

Dump, burn, or recycle

Over three-quarters of all waste produced worldwide is thrown into vast holes in the ground called **landfill** sites. Once one landfill site is full, then a new one is dug. Some of the rubbish gradually rots down making liquid called **leachate**. Leachate can **pollute** soil and water.

Other waste is burnt in enormous ovens called **incinerators**. This means less land is taken for landfill sites. The trouble is that burning releases polluting smoke and gases into the air.

A lot of waste including paper, metal cans, plastic bottles, and glass can be **recycled**. This means the material it is made from is reused. For example, used glass jars and bottles are crushed, melted, and moulded into new glass bottles. Other waste is used more directly. For example, people cut up old tyres to make sandals.

Breaking down

Bacteria can rot waste such as food, cotton cloth, and paper quickly in rubbish dumps. This waste is **biodegradable**. Other waste, such as plastic and metal, is non-biodegradable. This means it takes hundreds of years to rot. Our rubbish dumps fill up quickly and stay filled with non-biodegradable waste.

Piles of unwanted goods like these could take many thousands of years to biodegrade.

How much waste do we produce?

There are over 6 billion people on Earth. Each person produces about 400 kilograms (880 pounds) of rubbish each year. But this is an average amount. Some people create much more rubbish than others. The bar chart below compares how much waste each person produces each year in ten different countries. People in the USA produce the highest amount (720 kilograms or 1,580 pounds) and people in Mexico the lowest. But the numbers only compare countries whose governments are rich enough to collect waste. There are lots of countries whose people have no choice but to deal with their rubbish themselves.

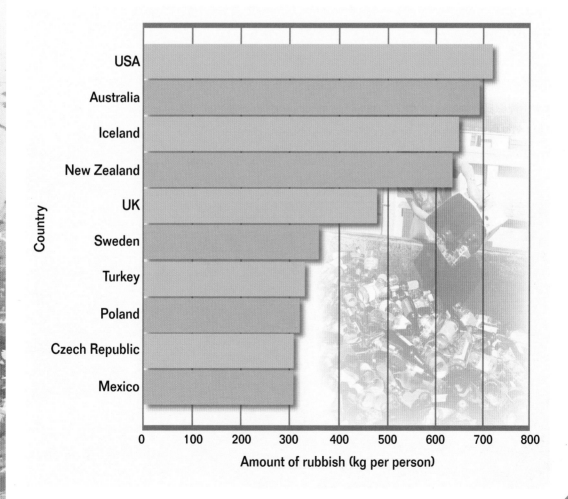

This bar chart compares the annual amount of rubbish per person in ten different countries.

{how does rubbish affect us?}

Rubbish is a big problem. Apart from looking horrible and smelling bad, it affects the **environment** and living things like us.

Rotting

Waste rots when **bacteria** feed on it. As they feed, numbers of bacteria increase. Some bacteria are harmful. For example, rotting disposable nappies contain human **faeces**. Faeces is solid waste from animals' bodies that contains bacteria and other germs. As faeces rots, these germs may get into **leachate**.

Leachate also contains dangerous fluids, such as **acid** leaked from batteries and bleach. Many **landfill** sites are lined with concrete to stop leachate soaking into the land around them. However, some sites are not lined and leachate may get into drinking water supplies. People who drink this **polluted** water can become sick.

*As the **population** increases and people buy more and more consumer goods, the amount of waste we produce piles up. The problem of how to deal with this waste is becoming a serious matter for countries around the world.*

Fuming

When bacteria rot waste, they produce a gas called methane. The world's landfill sites produce about 70 million tonnes (68 million tons) of methane each year. Methane is a gas that contributes to **global warming**.

When people burn waste such as plastics in **incinerators**, they release dangerous gases such as dioxin. In Japan, people who live nearest to waste incinerators can develop **cancer** after breathing in dioxin.

NIMBY recycling

What is NIMBY? Well, it is a word made up of the first letters of five words: Not In My Back Yard. Many countries in the world would rather not have to **recycle** their own waste in their own countries. It is expensive to collect and to build recycling factories to get rid of it. So they pack it into ships and send it to other countries where it costs less to deal with waste. But it usually passes on pollution problems to other places.

The stars on this map show the ports in Asia where Europe, Australia, and the USA send used computers for recycling. After being broken up and melted down, each computer produces about £3 worth of recycled material such as copper wire. But the process of getting at the valuable bits produces polluting gas and metal waste.

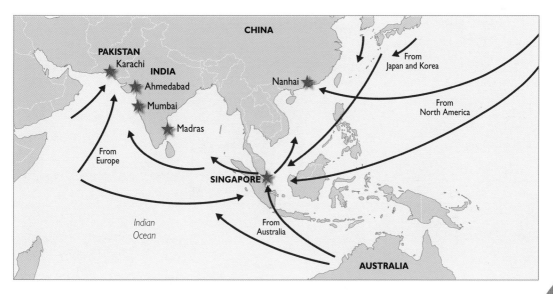

This map shows where waste computers end up for recycling.

{hazardous waste}

What do used gas bottles, unwanted bombs, and hospital waste have in common? They are all types of hazardous waste. Some hazardous waste, such as bombs and gas bottles, may explode and cause damage if heated up. So it should never be disposed of in **incinerators**. Hospital waste includes out-of-date medicines, which can make people sick if used in the wrong amounts. It includes used needles and scalpel blades that can cut and **infect** people who handle waste. Sharp, hazardous waste like this must be disposed of carefully in tough boxes.

Other hazardous waste can cause less obvious problems. Asbestos is a type of powdery rock used in buildings in the past. Asbestos powder contains extremely small, sharp fibres. If people breathe in these fibres, for example when they are working on old buildings, over time the fibres can damage their lungs.

Hazardous waste needs to be carefully handled and transported to stop it being spilled.

Long-lasting danger

Some hazardous waste remains a problem for tens of years. Strong poisons and nuclear waste (see box below) can be dangerous for a long time, even if only a small amount is spilled. To prevent it ever being spilled, this kind of waste is sealed in drums. These drums are stored in places where they should not be disturbed, such as at the bottom of oceans or down disused mine shafts. However, the drums need to be regularly checked to make sure they are undisturbed.

Nuclear waste

One way people make electricity is in nuclear power stations. They produce energy to make the electricity from special metal called uranium. Once the energy is released, the used uranium or nuclear waste is carefully removed. Nuclear waste is **radioactive**. This means it releases nuclear **radiation**, invisible gas, and rays that damage **cells** in our bodies causing **cancers**.

This diagram shows how nuclear waste is stored to stop it releasing radiation. First it is sealed in concrete or glass, inside thick metal drums. Then several drums are stored together in concrete buildings. Over time, the waste naturally becomes less radioactive. But this will take thousands of years.

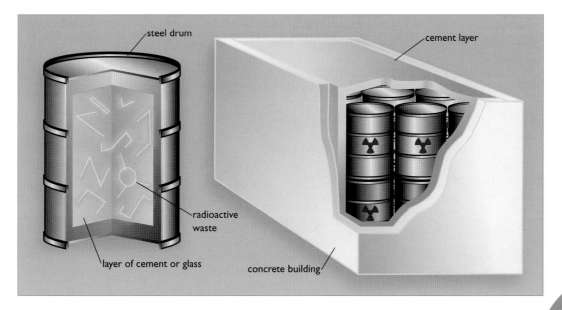

This diagram illustrates the storage method for nuclear waste.

{case study} Chernobyl

Very few people outside Russia had heard of a place called Chernobyl until 1986. On 26 April 1986, there was an accident in the nuclear power station at Chernobyl. So much energy was released from the nuclear fuel that it caused a gigantic fire. This caused some of the fuel to explode, blowing the heavy steel and concrete lid off the station. A massive cloud of **radioactive** dust escaped, which affected a large area of Europe.

Effects

The explosion at Chernobyl killed 30 people but it affected many more. At first, around 400,000 people fled from the areas closest to Chernobyl, where most radioactive waste had fallen. Over 400 villages where these people had lived were too radioactive for anyone to ever live in again. But many people returned to their homes in other villages and towns near Chernobyl. They were exposed to high amounts of **radiation**, when they breathed in radioactive dust or ate vegetables grown in radioactive soil. Since the accident, 2,500 people in the area around Chernobyl have died of **cancers** caused by the radiation. More are dying each year because the radiation is still having an effect.

Radioactive waste from Chernobyl was detected in sheep in Wales, over 1,500 kilometres (900 miles) from the accident site.

Radiation also affected the **environment** around Chernobyl. At first, forests of pine trees died and wildlife disappeared. But over time, as radioactive waste washed deeper into the soil, wildlife such as wolves, boar, and other animals returned to the area. Part of the reason they returned was because there were very few people about.

Spreading radioactivity

After the Chernobyl accident, most radioactivity was found nearest the power station. Then the radioactive cloud high in the sky was blown around by winds. This meant that smaller, less dangerous amounts spread across Europe. These maps show where radioactive waste from Chernobyl was detected in the nine days after the accident. Map 2 shows how at first the radioactive cloud was detected north of Chernobyl. Maps 3 and 4 show that it gradually spread south over the Mediterranean Sea.

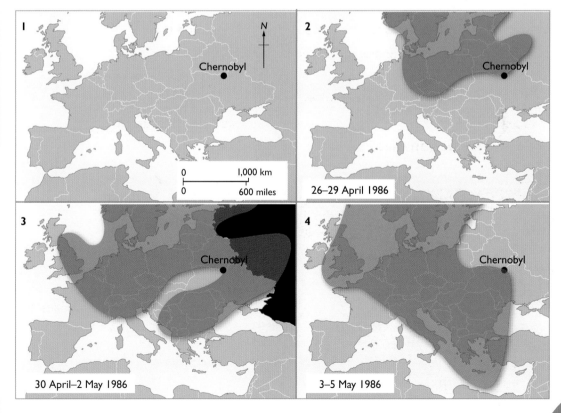

These maps show areas affected by the Chernobyl nuclear disaster.

{the world's wild places}

Where in the world does waste **pollute**? The answer is almost everywhere. The worst effects of waste pollution are often closest to where people live. But waste affects even wild places, the remotest parts of Earth where very few people live.

Some waste that is dropped from ships or blown off land washes around the world's oceans. Much of this waste, such as chunks of polystyrene, plastic bottles, and ripped fishing nets, is not **biodegradable**. This kind of waste can also harm marine animals. For example, dolphins and seals may get tangled in old nets and then not be able to hunt for food.

FACT!

Three-quarters of all the waste floating in the world's oceans is plastic.

Many people visit Nepal to walk and climb in the dramatic Himalayan Mountains. Sadly some of them leave piles of waste such as plastic water bottles and other rubbish that local people have to clean up.

Floating waste may wash up on shores hundreds of kilometres from where it was dropped. The beaches of even the tiniest uninhabited islands in the middle of the Pacific Ocean, such as Henderson Island, are dotted with litter.

Parting gift

Visitors leave waste in wild places. Some people visit wild places to work, for example to find new supplies of oil or timber they need. Tourists visit wild places to get close to amazing wildlife, scenery, and different cultures. Some of these visitors leave waste such as used bottles and cooking gas canisters, broken flip-flops, and empty suncream tubes. It looks horrible and also leaves a problem for others to clear up.

Leather back turtles are under threat. One of the main reasons is that they die from eating plastic bags in the oceans. They eat them because floating bags look a bit like jellyfish, one of their favourite foods.

{why do we need wild places?}

Wild places are very important to our planet's health. They are not only home to a wide variety of types of plant and animals, but also vital parts of the global **environment**.

Wildlife

Wild places include remote mountains and deserts, deep oceans, and wide forests and marshes. When people **pollute** or damage these wild places they may injure or kill individual plants and animals that live there. Pollution sometimes damages whole communities of **interdependent** living things.

An area of tropical rainforest the size of New York City is being chopped down each day somewhere in the world.

The importance of trees

All animals eat food but they need **oxygen** to release energy from it. Land animals like us breathe in oxygen from the **atmosphere**. Lake, river, and ocean animals take in oxygen that is dissolved in the water. As they use oxygen, animals produce **carbon dioxide** waste. Trees and other plants use up carbon dioxide and make oxygen (see box below). Without plants there would be no oxygen and the atmosphere would also contain far too much carbon dioxide.

People are cutting down large areas of the world's forests to clear land and to sell the wood. With fewer trees, less carbon dioxide is being removed from the atmosphere. As the balance of gases in the atmosphere changes, **global warming** will speed up and the hole in the **ozone layer** will open further.

Making oxygen, taking carbon dioxide

Green plants make oxygen (O_2) through **photosynthesis**. This is a special process powered by the Sun's energy that happens in leaves. The diagram below reminds us that carbon dioxide (CO_2) comes from animals that breathe it out and from burning **fossil fuels**. It illustrates how carbon dioxide gas from the atmosphere and water from the ground enter leaves. Inside each leaf these ingredients are jumbled up and re-formed into sugar and oxygen. Plants use sugar as food and release oxygen into the atmosphere.

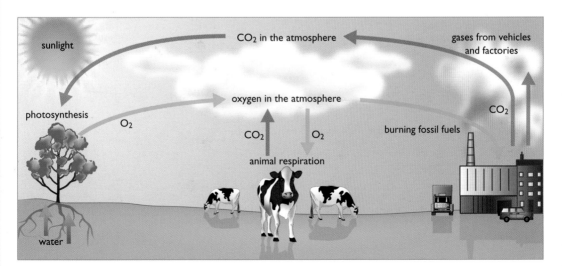

This diagram shows the balance between trees taking in carbon dioxide, and cars and factories pumping it out.

{investigating environmental change}

It is sometimes obvious when a part of the **environment** is **polluted**. A cloud of grey-brown **smog** hanging over a city is a clue that the air is polluted. However, many changes in the environment are not always so easy to spot. For example, polluted water may look crystal clear.

Monitoring

Scientists with specialist knowledge of different parts of the environment monitor pollution. This means they check up to see whether it is happening and what effects it is having. For example, some scientists take regular measurements of the amounts of polluting gases in the **atmosphere**. The scientists work for governments and other organizations such as **conservation** groups. These organizations use the scientists' data to work out how dangerous the environmental change is. They can then take action to control that change.

Conservation groups and pollution

How do conservation groups help protect the environment from pollution?

- They **campaign** for changes in laws controlling how much pollution factories produce.

- They tell people which industries and individuals are causing pollution.

- They help set up and maintain nature reserves, which are wild places where wildlife and plants live protected from people.

- They have websites and send out leaflets warning people about the dangers of pollution.

POPs star!

Paul Johnston works for the conservation group Greenpeace in the freezing Arctic environment. His job is to monitor the amounts of polluting chemicals called POPs that are found there.

Paul measures the amounts of POPs found in seawater, in ice, and in marine animals. For example, he catches fish and measures POPs in their blood. He also examines different **tissues** from dead seals that Greenpeace find.

Using information provided by scientists like Paul Johnston, Greenpeace have discovered that POPs are found all over the Arctic, even though it is a wild place where very few people live. They have also found that the largest amounts of POPs build up in the thick fatty tissue that protects Arctic seals from the cold.

Scientist Paul Johnston at work, providing information for Greenpeace.

{the future: reversing the changes?}

The future for the **environment** is difficult to predict. We have seen how many parts of the environment are at risk, mostly as a result of people's **pollution**. So how do we make things better for us all?

The simple answer is people must find ways of reducing pollution. There are lots of things people are doing around the planet right now. Some people are using alternatives to **fossil fuels** that do not pollute. For example, they are making electricity using the Sun's energy in **solar cells**. Some people are finding ways of reducing waste. For example, they make computers that are easier to **recycle** and create less hazardous waste.

Working together

Governments of many countries are working together to reduce pollution. The Kyoto Protocol is an agreement to release fewer **carbon dioxide** and other polluting gases into the atmosphere. Some countries that make a lot of pollution, such as the USA and Australia, have not yet signed the Kyoto Protocol. We all need to look after our world environment much more to ensure a good future for the environment.

Cars without fossil fuels

Cars are already being made whose engines produce virtually no polluting gases. Some burn alcohol fuel made from sugar cane or farm waste. Some use special batteries that run on liquid hydrogen, which can be made from seawater. What comes out of the exhaust pipe in each case is water.

Make a difference

We can all do our bit to help the environment. Here are just a few ideas:

- Take part in clearing up litter from your street, your school or your local beach. Make sure the litter is disposed of properly.

- Make less waste, for example choose food with less packaging and use **rechargeable** batteries in your gadgets.

- Walk and cycle more! You will feel fitter and what's more, less oil will be used and less air pollution will be made by vehicles.

- Use less electricity, for example by turning off lights and TVs. Remember most electricity is made by burning fossil fuels.

One way to help the environment is by taking part in a group litter clean-up.

{further resources}

Books

Kingfisher Knowledge: Endangered Planet, David Burnie (Kingfisher, 2004)

Taking Action: Friends of the Earth, Louise Spilsbury (Heinemann Library, 2000)

What's at Issue: Making a Difference, Richard Spilsbury (Heinemann Library, 2002)

Websites

You can explore the Internet to find out more about pollution. Websites can change, so if the links below no longer work use a reliable search engine.

To find out more about air pollution and what you can do to prevent some of it go to http://edugreen.teri.res.in/explore/air/air.htm.

To find out more about the ozone layer go to http://science.howstuffworks.com/ozone-pollution.htm.

The UK site www.environment-agency.gov.uk/fun has lots of games and information about environmental issues.

This UK site has lots of helpful information about water pollution: http://www.ukrivers.net/pollution.html.

Air Pollution: What's the Solution? is an educational project for young people at http://www.k12science.org/curriculum/airproj/.

At www.coolkidsforacoolclimate.co/Explained/Kyotoprotocol there is a clear and full explanation of what the Kyoto Protocol is all about.

Conservation organizations

Lots of conservation groups have websites with information about looking after the environment.

Visit http://www.panda.org/kids, the website of the World Wide Fund for Nature. The site has information on lots of wildlife and environment issues and games such as 'Toxic Blaster'.

Visit Friends of the Earth websites to learn more about their projects:
www.foe.co.uk (Friends of the Earth, UK)
www.foe.org.au (Friends of the Earth, Australia).

{glossary}

acid a strong chemical that can burn or damage things

acid rain rainwater that has been polluted by chemicals in the air, making it acidic and damaging to wildlife

asthma when people find it hard to breathe properly

atmosphere layers of air that surround planet Earth

bacteria tiny living things found everywhere, in air, water, soils, and food. Some bacteria are good for us; others can cause disease.

biodegradable something that breaks down and rots away easily

campaign using advertisements, public appearances, and debates to help make people aware of a particular issue, such as environmental damage

cancer disease in which abnormal cells grow and spread. Cancer can be fatal.

carbon dioxide invisible gas found in the Earth's atmosphere

cell smallest building block of all living things

climate general conditions of weather in an area

conservation protecting and saving wildlife and parts of the natural world such as rivers

diarrhoea illness that makes your faeces liquid and makes you go to the toilet very often. Each time you go, you lose water from your body.

earthquake when part of the surface of the Earth suddenly moves

environment our surroundings: the air, land, and sea in which we live

erupts when a volcano suddenly shoots out lava and ash

faeces solid waste

fertilizers chemical powders, sprays, or liquids used to improve soil and help plants grow

flood when water overflows its banks and washes onto dry areas of land

fossil fuel fuels such as oil, coal, and gas. They formed from the remains of plants and animals that lived millions of years ago. They cannot be replaced.

global warming rise in temperatures across the world, caused by the greenhouse effect (blanket of gases in the air that are trapping heat)

ice cap area permanently covered in ice, such as found at Poles

incinerators large ovens for burning waste

infect to pass on a disease

interdependent when living things rely on each other for life in some way

landfill site where waste is dumped in a big hole and covered with soil

leachate black liquid that forms as waste rots

oil tanker huge ocean-going ship used to transport oil

oxygen gas in the atmosphere that living things need to breathe in order to live

ozone layer layer of gas in the atmosphere that absorbs harmful rays of sunlight

pesticides chemicals used to kill insects and other crop pests

photosynthesis process by which plants make food in their leaves, using water, carbon dioxide from the air, and energy from sunlight

pollution something that poisons or damages air, water, or land in a way that can harm people's health or the environment

population number of people

radiation movement of energy in the form of rays or waves we cannot see, such as heat and light from the Sun

radioactive when something is giving off harmful radiation

raw material material found in nature, such as oil, soil or rock, which is used to make something else

rechargeable energy source that can be recharged when it has run out

recycled when waste is changed into something that can be used again, for example when old glass bottles are made into new ones

reefs ridges of rock or coral at or near the surface of the sea

reservoir man-made lake for storing water

satellite object in space that sends out TV signals or takes photographs

sewage human waste carried away from people's homes in drains

smog when sunlight mixes with smoke and other air pollution

solar cell device that uses the Sun's energy for making electricity

species single, distinct class of living thing with features that distinguish it from others

tissue group of cells that has a particular function in a body. For example, skin cells grow together to form skin tissue

ultraviolet radiation rays that come to the Earth from the Sun, which are invisible but can cause sunburn

volcano when hot liquid rock from the centre of the Earth spurts out from a hole in the Earth's crust

{index}